The Speaker Within

The Wisdoms of Adrian Crawford

www.theworksofadriancrawford.com

Published in Australia by Sid Harta Books & Print Pty Ltd,
ABN: 34632585293
23 Stirling Crescent, Glen Waverley, Victoria 3150 Australia
Telephone: +61 3 9560 9920
E-mail: author@sidharta.com.au

First published in Australia 2021
This edition published 2021
Copyright © Adrian Crawford 2021
Cover design, typesetting: WorkingType (www.workingtype.com.au)

Cover artwork: commissioned artwork by D. J Stief, 1996,
inspired by the author's photographic collage.

The right of Adrian Crawford to be identified as the
Author of the Work has been asserted in accordance with the
Copyright, Designs and Patents Act 1988.

All rights reserved. No part of this publication may be reproduced, stored in a retrieval system, or transmitted, in any form or by any means without the prior written permission of the publisher, nor be otherwise circulated in any form of binding or cover other than that in which it is published and without a similar condition being imposed on the subsequent purchaser.

Crawford, Adrian
The Speaker Within — The Wisdoms of Adrian Crawford
ISBN: 978-1-925707-62-5
pp124

Dedication

*This book is dedicated with love to
my immediate Crawford family.
To those no longer with us, my sister, Hilary,
whose courage touched so many,
to my father, Norman Frank Crawford
for his great wit and inspiration,
to my mother, Molly Crawford,
for her deep passion and advocacy of conservation
for most of her ninety-eight years.
And also, to all those who continue to share the journey,
To Jon, Gill and to my wife, Sherlz.
And finally, to my fellow author and eldest brother,
David (Dave), without who this book may never have reached
the light of day.*

Preface

Firstly, welcome to *The Speaker Within*, a collection of my inspirational sayings. I commenced the odyssey of writing this book in September 1989. With the inclusion of previously uncompiled material, it was gradually completed over a seven-year period. In this updated edition, I have added several additional sayings but the bulk of the text remains the same. Mused upon a bush trail, soliloquised in the bathtub, conjured in a conversation, spun in a dream, or inspired from a Reiki healing. Such are the different ways that these sayings came into being. Most often, they reflect either on my own growth or on what I most needed to learn. Many are absorbed and reconjugated from a variety of sources. And yet, nearly all originate through what I came to regard as *The Speaker Within*.

You may decide to voyage through this collection by reading from beginning to end or by meditating on the sayings you find pertinent. You could also consider formulating a question that you want answering, then delving inside to see what is revealed. The choice is yours.

And now, to overleaf for an answer to what,

or who is my 'Speaker Within'.

Intuition:

Tuition from within.

Contents

Dedication	iii
Preface	v
Changes	1
Humankind	5
On Life	8
Learners All	11
Love	13
And Love's Opportunity	15
The Spiritual Journeyer	21
The Essence Spirituality	25
Earth Purpose	32
To a Cause Committed	36
Conflict	38
Autumn Seasons	40
Letting Go	42
Hurdles	46
Patterns	49
Of Self-esteem Depleted	51
Future Clouded / Path Divided	53

Be Still	57
Correcting Your Course	58
A Step to the Lateral	61
Support	63
...And Gratitude.	65
Compassion Seeds	67
Healing Balm	69
Growing Greater Acceptance	72
Accepting Others	75
Experience	77
Wisdom's Song	79
Of Essence	80
The Child Within	87
Fun	89
Beauty	91
Just Be	93
The Next Step	94
On Track	96
Guiding Others	97
On Mastery	98
Discovery	99
Creed of the Evolution	101
...And a Final Thought	111
Epilogue	112
Acknowledgements:	113
About the Author	114

Changes

Life is like a river

flowing to the ocean

for the very first time.

As the river journeys forth,

does it lament the dried river beds

it could have chosen but instead passed by?

Or does it relish the discovery of each new day

as it flows headstrong upon its course?

The Way of Change can be

a tumultuous pummelling,

cascading you down ravines unbidden.

The Way of Change can be

the swift surging of a river,

flow-arrowed upon its mission.

The Way of Change can be

a sluggish ripple,

stagnating alone in back-watered limbo.
The Way of Change can be
a lake, still and inner,
content with its belonging to the All.
The Way of Change is all, or many, or none,
For such it is:
the Soul Flow...

By fighting to change a behaviour,
you ensure its continuance:
For the defensive walls that surround that behaviour
were built to protect your innermost beliefs.
Is it any wonder the gates do not open
to a persecuting army?
Love and flow with that behaviour
and thank it for all it has served you.
And one day, when it looks beyond its battlements
and sees not a besieging army,
but only peace and harmony in the Land,
then the gates can be opened
and the walls slowly dissolve.

Even if for one second
you became aware
that you are someone worthwhile:
it counts!
For a second can become a minute,
an hour, a day, a lifetime.
All it takes
is that moment.

Change does not have to be uphill,
straining hard against an unyielding object.
It can be the gentlest of breezes,
whispering softly to the profoundest of depths.

Your most negative belief
threw you back on your own inner resources;
caused you to grow and develop in ways
which you likely would not have,
had all your needs been met;
So thank it, love yourself for it
and
change.

And we, every one of us,

are loving, powerful beings.

All we have to do

is

choose.

With what immensity of power

we each create our lives!

Thus, when we focus on change,

the extraordinary is within our grasp.

To know is to realise that

though we can support change in others,

it is they who must ultimately decide.

Change

changes everything.

Humankind

As lightning forks the pitch darkness in a cataclysm of white,
and waves uplift great arms of worshipful foam
towards the moon,
We belong.

As the sun rises through the mist-orbed dawn,
and with joyous song, flighted birds greet a new awakening,
We belong.

As the Earth spins its galactic course,
And humanity swirls a myriad path of discovery unfolding,
We belong.

We belong, from the youngest to the most ancient;
from the richest to the most destitute;
from the wisest to the most lost;
from the cruellest to the most loving.
For whosoever, or whatever, we are:
We all belong.

Look around you and know,
that of everyone you see,
there is but one simple truth:
We are all capable of Love.

With everything we are in relationship:
With ourselves and our bodies,
with others of all nations,
and with the Earth itself.
And communication and sensitivity;
that which maintain the harmony.
For only through connection's lack does crisis occur.
Yet within every crisis lies also
the key to healing.

Upon this Earth has arisen many a mountain,

Atop each mountain, trickles formed from falling rain,

down to join as Stream the trickles all did flow.

Onwards to a River, the many streams next coursed,

till into the one Ocean, all the rivers finally outpoured.

Now imagine all waters are the Rivers of Humanity;

And at the very point tumultuous where

all Rivers do meet the Ocean –

that is where we are

in humanity's story.

On Life

Life is like a flower,
opening and unfurling its undewed petals
towards the dawning light.

We are learners all
on the playground of experience.

Life is a tide that ebbs and flows.
When your life is flow, expand, reach out, explore!
For, by so doing, you will learn the most.
But when your life is ebb, draw back, contract
to the very Source of your being.
For that too,
is where you most need to be...

Every moment is precious.

Embrace your loves,

your passion,

and your every experience

like it is now and forever.

You are a gift of life,

to life itself.

(So can I join in the celebration?)

You did not get the experience of a lifetime

to not experience that lifetime to the full.

If you are going to live,

you are going to get older.

Life is a most profound collaboration.

Grasp it.

Enjoy

and in joy,

be in love with life!

Learners All

If you learn with the will of a child
as it walks for the very first time,
then no endeavour
will be beyond your grasp.

At any given moment you have in your life
only those who have the most to teach you.
If someone does not stay, it is because
they are no longer the ideal person to learn from;
irrespective of how much you, or they,
want that connection maintained.

The greatest of teachers continually appreciate
that, though the guise may be different,
the learning is always mutual.

I cannot teach you anything
you do not already know.
You are simply relearning what you need
for the next step upon your path.

You _always_ make the right decisions!
Even if
you do have to learn from them...

Immaturity is to a tree
what maturity is to a sapling.
There is no time limit:
Only the perfect Age.

Every Age is perfect
for what you need to learn.

Love

Love is always there,
it's just patiently waiting for us
to turn around
and notice it.

Inside us all; is an enormous well of love.
Hoard it, and we deny not only ourselves that love,
but we disavow each and every person
we meet.

In the ever vastness of Love,
pain and perfectionism have no place;
for separateness can no more exist within union,
than fear within Love.

What lies at the root
of all experience?

Love yourself

If you are forever searching for love,
but never finding it,
it is because
you have never lost it...

Energy is love,
and everything is energy.
Thus love is everywhere
when we open our eyes to see.

And Love's Opportunity

Love starts with a relationship with ourselves,
and expands
outwards...

People are like ships upon a sea,
and a relationship is their meeting.
Many do pass each other by,
but a couple can form from the meeting of two.
Two ships travelling together; sometimes close,
at times more apart.
And though each may steer a different course,
together they may sail upon a lifetime's journey.

The more that you reveal of yourself
with openness and honesty,
the more there is for another to love.

A relationship can flow, ebb, grow, and change.
So why analyse each nuance
when you can enjoy what it has to offer?

Good communication is the gravitational field
that holds a relationship
in orbit.

Be careful of entering a relationship
desirous of changing another.
Respect that they are their own perfection
and need not your redesigning.

Behind a desire to control
is a deep fear of love,
and in a relationship lies the challenge
to go beyond...

And Love's Opportunity

Dependency is someone living in terror
that one day
they may have to love themselves.

When you love too much
you give your all and avoid receiving.
And in the dance called intimacy,
your one hand be outstretched,
the other lock-held against your heart,
fear-protective of true closeness.
And to you, most likely, will come such
who will take your all, and the giving avoid;
for a likewise fear claws them in its grip.
But when of Self you love, and of joy, love another,
the dance does change, as too the partner,
and there will arrive one, of as great a love.
Now both your hands will flow together,
touch gentle of hand upon a mutual heart
as softly enjoined in give and take,
you move the Dance Intuitive,
the energy dance
of Love.

When in a relationship, you are locked in unforgiveness,
free of them you will never truly be; for your hands
are metaphysically locked around their throat.
And too easily will you be drawn to the same person
as the one you never forgave.
Only by forgiveness can you at last break the pattern,
set yourself free and open yourself up
to someone entirely new.

Only a giver willing to be loved,
will attract another giver
open to receive.

A relationship is not so much
what you expect it's going to be
as what you most need to learn...

Balance in love,
as in all things,
is the only way of harmony.

If you are not in a relationship,
bemoan not this lack,
but relish this opportunity for aloneness.
Treat yourself as intimately as you would a lover:
For it is when we are happy with ourselves,
within or without a relationship,
that truly balanced, interdependent intimacy
can develop between ourselves and others.

The more we love and nurture
our own inner child,
the more likely we are to attract
relationships both positive and healthy.

You can search all your life to find
that beautiful someone,
till the moment you find
that beautiful someone within.
Then you are ready to meet
that beautiful someone
who has also discovered
Self.

I deserve the best for me
and you deserve the best for you,
and if we become friends,
then the best we are for each other.

Every new relationship:
The seed
of a never-before beginning.

A wonderful gift is the love for each other
generated by two in intimacy.
Yet even greater can be the blossoming,
when constantly reaffirmed.
So, honour and communicate your love
as oft you can.
For that which is most cherished
will only grow the stronger.

Relish and flow
with mutual accord,
upon the journey of Love.

The Spiritual Journeyer

I am aloneness, solitary, unique.
I am the immutable, yet ever changeable:
Many waters flow against me, move me,
build me up, take me down.
Yet constant the inner flame remains,
enfolded in a million imprints,
belonging only to one, and yet, to all:
For I am...
that is.

Spirituality and sexuality:
There is no duality,
only being.

Beyond sexual gratification
is the love that can merge two people
into the God-like transcendence
that is

Oneness.

Insight:
Clarity of the Spirit
on the road to union.

To draw an analogy from physics:
If we are one per cent matter,
and ninety-nine per cent space,
then religion is the one per cent
and the spiritual is the other...

(see over page).

One hundred per cent.

(See the previous page).

Structure is man-made,

Spirit isn't.

But the seeker after enlightenment may well need the steps
that structure provides to reach the heightened pinnacle.

Yet to merge with the Spiritual sun,

transcended

is the cocoon of mere understanding.

Let go of your spiritual constipation

in your search for ultimate truth.

For the truly spiritually enlightened

just _know_ how to have fun!

Trust

the God flow...

Life is all a spiritual path,

And we the journeyers on it...

The Essence Spirituality

The Essence of maleness/femaleness has in the East
long been known, and in the West by Jung proclaimed
Tantra, Anima, Animus, Yin and Yang are the
names to it given.
Yet not of intellect was Essence born, for it is energy raw,
of aspect dual, that humans, men and women both,
have within their being.

The aspect feminine is passion in aliveness, inner-knowing
exactly what she wants.
Loving, sexual, of the Goddess she is hailed.
Initiator of energy masculine, care tender of
intuition and creation; she is the compassion
that unites us to Spirit.

The masculine aspect of which I speak is just as much
an energy within, and of the feminine a partner spiritual equal.
Lion-like, desirous of letting roar is the Inner Masculine;
eyes beholden with piercing clarity: no goal wells
beyond his grasp.

Yet immense is his good nature, aggression marring not his step
as with great humour, play, joy and love he does her bidding.
For it is the Inner Feminine, who, from the deeper Wisdom,
intuits the path.

Fiery and boundless the love they bear our being;
twin flames, they curl together in the beauty of union,
making of a human a greater one.
For they are the Inner Beloved,
the aspects unifying of Spirit emergent.

To feel this awareness potent within your breast
is to know confidence that soars,
for this state be, for man and for woman, the perfection
of our power, our love and our beauty,
the wholeness at last.

Fear of homosexuality is the mirage that keeps us
from truly loving our own beingness, physical and sexual;
for how can we self-love when of the same gender we belong?
Hindered from claiming the fullness of our power,
obstructed too is the love-bond for like gender kin and friends.
And all the while masked is the deeper terror:
Loving connection with the aspect gender opposite within,
who bears an attraction primal and healing
to the totality of our own gender selves.

Be not afraid of shining a light on areas dim,
for any shadows feared and repressed can be absorbed
by joyously honouring of Self, bringing with it
a deeper completeness.
And the heart-core of our orientation sexual will remain
unchanged as we merge with the duality-as-one
of our Inner Beloved so gently awaiting
what it has always desired:
our loving, in every aspect,
who we were born to be.

Love your own gender self.
Seeing the Divine within the temple of your own body,
And you will absolutely be loved in return.

Life cannot continue to exist without sex,
so cherish its glorious sharing.
Especially as, with maturing, you both attain
a higher plane of love and spiritual melding.

The expression of sexuality
is but peripheral
to the potential for love
beckoning at its core.

More alike than culture-bound roles would allow, are
men and women both, and to the Women's Movement
goes much credit in freeing us.

Yet more than ever, a new ideal is needed, beyond mimicry
unintended of the cultural extremes of the other gender
and calling it growth,
For such is likewise unattuned to either inner aspect.
Merely a new form of the shackles of old
that have kept the gender concerned for timeless generations
not adults true, but hurt and angry children grown.

Beyond ego-lures that only empower separateness within
and without we need to go to an evolution down
the path of greatest growth
to when the masculine and feminine inside both the genders
will be at last in synergy; at one with the Inner Beloved.

Then men and women will find the natural balance
between them; softness for some, powerfulness for others,
whatever the individual suits:
For the genders have always overlapped.
And those who are strongly masculine or feminine will feel
the more so.
Yet power will be with love and softness with strength.
And not misused but instead respected, by men and by women,
will be the aspect masculine.

And whatever their orientation, both genders would have
high self-esteem, accepting only an Equal in balanced,
deep and very loving relationship.
For no one would seek to possess another for the aspect
gender opposite they once felt they lacked,
for they now experience the love inside themselves
of both their aspects.

And to understand homosexuality from the inner and
loving sight as to their own gender potent, all the while
of spiritual fire is to relinquish the fear.
Letting grow in its stead greater trust of one's own gender.
As men and women discover within themselves
an intuitive Self that needs no approval,
reconnecting with the awesome gentleness of the Inner Beloved,
they enter Initiation: into manhood, into womanhood, reclaiming
the very spiritual rightness of their gender birthed.

And now Men and Women can at last embrace one another
in true understanding of who they always have been
- beneath the illusion.

If ever there was a time in history for men and women to come
into the truth of who they are, it is now.
The masculine energy of old, ego-driven, culturally defined;
defences so high that of the Inner Feminine never hears,
has led us pell-mell into our world plight.
But now, the energy beyond measure of the Inner Feminine
spiralling towards consummation is impelling a new
ecological awareness and spiritual reawakening as she summons
the masculine energy to heed her call for change
before it is too late.

Beyond the powerlessness of blame or of guilt,
men and women needs go; to the power of responsibility:
to a time of great healing,
forging a new link and communicating as equals
for the love of each other and survival of Mother Earth.
So, let us, men and women, be teacher and pupil both
as we journey upon this road together.

Earth Purpose

Nature weaves its web of power;
potent harmony its every breath.
Loom the crisis of our folly,
and opportunity flows in danger's wake.
Now the hands will join together;
Global Wisdom in survival's name.
And so begins the Healing.

Tomorrow's future:
Born of today.

Doing for ourselves and humanity
at one and the same time
(and not one or the other),
is one of the greatest lessons
that humanity needs to learn.

We are at the foothills of a Great Evolution
with the tide below us rising.
Either humanity will choose as a body
to step to a higher plane,
or we will be swept away by the effluent tide
of our own creating.

We who are alive
are the privileged,
Born at a time of greatest crises,
to make a difference.

If the way we treat ourselves is the way we treat the Earth,
then we had better look
at what we're doing…

A glimmer of dawn the New Age can reveal,
But a far greater Dawn must arise
when all branches of human endeavour,
transcend, transform, to work as One,
for the birth
of Planethood.

The feminine and masculine dance within us all
a duet of energy and power.
The feminine guides, the masculine heeds,
and together as one, they can heal this Earth.

Earth and Spirit:
The Guardianship of this, our Planet,
is the true mantle
of the New Millennium.

When the need is greatest,
the Greatest arise.

Is humanity hovering
on the *very verge*
of Global...

(see over page)

Maturity?

(See the previous page)

To a Cause Committed

Do that which needs be done.

If you anger for your cause,
you create 'them' and 'us'.
But love that cause,
and there is only 'us'.

Great deeds can be done
under the burden of obligation.
But far greater still can be achieved
under the aegis of love.

If you have a cause,
care about it so much
that your love for it is great enough
to lap even the portals
of those who most oppose you.

If you see a wrong that must be righted,
write it.

Conflict

When someone vents their anger,
the fool diverges into the line of fire.
The wise continue upon their path.

Any anger is always hurt
crying out for love and understanding.

When someone flares at another's opinion;
what insecurity must it challenge in them?
For if you trust and value what you hold true
then accepted with ease is many a view
without ever the one being jeopardised.

Conflict

When two powerful rivers meet,
do they spend their time and effort
trying to force the other
back upon its course?
Or do they resolve their conflict
and head towards the sea?

Without conflict,
there might be
no resolution.

Harmony in conflict:
Synergy in motion...

Autumn Seasons

Life is brimmed full of changing season;
abounding with joy, sorrow, beauty and pain,
not one will Nature's course disdain.

For those who do cry, and let it be many,
feel not alone, for I cry too.
Tears are like leaves shed in an Autumn of sorrows;
waterfalled, rain-born 'tis nature's dew.

Loneliness is a state of mind -
not a state of the heart.

Why regret?
Your ability to do
is always here.

Life begets,

never regrets,

the soul's progression.

Love the inner child, for it is crying.

Comfort and cherish it and allow the time for grieving:

For beneath your hurt exists always the opportunity

to love yourself that bit more.

And once it accepts that it is loved, your inner child

will help you in every way to grow

into that beautiful, loving, confident being

that is your birthright.

Letting Go

Let go of the tense controlling of outcomes;
of feasting on future fear, on past remorse
and conclusions self-negating.
For when we learn to trust the intuitive guidance,
recognising in the synchronicity of people and events
drawn to us, a well-spring of spiritual flow,
we are connecting to a life of
empowerment and fulfilment.

By living our lives on past experience,
we recreate only the limitations that have been,
not the future that will be.
For power is ever present,
not ever past...

Do not justify, do not blame, for they lead
not to healing change,
but to the disowning of true power
in the cause of past anger,
and the continuance of separateness,
not the healing of wounds.
And such was never the path of responsibility.

Forgiveness, healing and letting go of the past,
however hard they may seem,
are always better
than being locked in anger.

As the Buddha within might say:
Forgiveness is a powerful weapon
in the armament of love.

If you cling to your past foundations,
you are clutched to your roots,
when the sun always challenges you to grow.

Out of all seeming failures
can emerge the greatest
of never-before
opportunities.

A healthy ego
does not cling to the outer frame
of a closed door.

Would a bird be able to fly,
an otter be able to swim,
a child be able to walk,
if fear ruled every endeavour?

Though by rocky slide taken,
no mountaineer would let their mind dwell
on the mountain's base,
when to look up is to see the summit,
and begin to climb anew.

Letting Go

When there is a letting-go,
natural and necessary
is the totality of grief.
Be at the utmost, gentle and loving.
And know that after the longing night,
Comes always a new day.

Letting go,
in all its forms,
creates the space
for something new.

Hurdles

Narcissism is to self-love
merely a mocking half-shadow.
Closer kin of self-hatred it be and for both,
a dreaded fear of belonging.
But self-love knows no such boundary.
From the greatest to the smallest,
it connects to the All.

Believe in the key, and the door will open.
But believe only in the lock
And you have forsaken it.

There is innocence in the greatest of cynics.
Cynicism is the mind
temporarily disconnected from the heart
in order to learn its lessons there.
But Heart and Spirit are innocent and eternal
and gently await the mind's return.

If you are to pain addicted, trust and let go.
For without emotional pain, there is room inside
left only for that you greatest fear:

Love.

All the praise in the world will mean nothing,
Till the moment you give in
and allow the love inside
the right to be you.

The seed of commitment can only open and grow
when the clouds of discontent part
and let the sun shine in.

If you are like an eagle that soars high
above a mountain top, ever afraid to land,
look to your heart, for the eagle never of courage lacked.
And with desire manifest, timing perfect, you will clear
the fear-illusioned raging storm that lies before your eyes,
shedding in its wake feelings old and painful.
Now afire with greater vision, you plummet,
down to the nest always there awaiting.

If you wallow only in the mire of hatred, pain and suffering
in the World,
then you commit to nothing, achieve nothing and leave
nothing.
But focus on the love, the healing and the joy,
and bring that in any and every way into your life and into
the lives of others,
Then there will be no limit to the effect you create.

To give up hope
is to deny the possible.

Patterns

If your pattern doesn't serve you...
change it!

Blame, justification, guilt and self-punishment
are not the path of maturity,
simply the patterns the child did learn.

Self-punishment:
The energy of fear
disguised as improvement.

Desire is energy in cycle.
Express it,
and it will complete.
Suppress it, deeply repress it,

and it will control you.
In endless cycle locked will be
the energies of desire and fear.
Yet by loving acknowledgement
the pattern completes,
even if fulfilment the desire never meets.

The baggage of guilt can clutter the heart,
and freeze with fear the spontaneous
possibilities of encounter new.
Unleash the joy held in trammel by such feelings old,
respond to situation fresh with fledgling steps;
and lovingly embrace your vulnerability.

Guilt is merely fear, past-centred;
disempowering this moment
from the potential for change.

Of Self-esteem Depleted

How much pain are you willing to endure
to finally realise you are truly worthy of love?

Health is not living under the eternal shadow
of others' disapproval.
Health is stepping out from under those shadows.
And on a level not conscious, even those
who most oppress this, could ask
for nothing more...

Guilt is merely fear, past-centred;
disempowering this moment of immense power
from the potential for change.

Your awesome potential
is not what has been,
but the unfathomed
waiting to be used.

Belittle not the tiniest achievement.
For why nip the first bud of an oak in seed?

If you honestly acknowledge
what you experience,
then this is _your_ truth.
To no one need you prove it.

From this very moment
all is ready
to start anew.

Be the magnet
of your own worth.

Future Clouded / Path Divided

When your head demands that this is your direction —

Wait.

When others expect that you should follow —

Wait.

When you want love so much; what they want,

you will tell them —

Wait.

Wait

for that gentlest voice

which blossoms and will nurture you,

which enlivens and will energise you.

Wait

and you will know it.

When you are at a stage of unresolved possibilities
(sometimes known as confusion!),
persist not for instant answers when none forthcome,
but enjoy the realm of the possible.
And in its own right time,
the answer will be clear.

Your expectations of where you want to go
may well be clouding your intuition
of where you need to go.

Stop!
Listen to what is in your heart to do,
for that is where the wisdom lies.

The World can go on without us.
But we can't.

What you think will happen -

may not.

What needs to happen...

will.

Working for security may acknowledge your fears.

But...

does it acknowledge your innermost desires?

Towards their goal grow some like a pine;

Singularly focused upon their purpose.

Yet others like a shrub do branch

on not one road, but many a path.

For these others to whom I most relate,

flow with the energy wherever it takes.

And upon a time unique,

all will be revealed...

The Speaker Within

If I gave you a seed and you knew not what it was,

and I told you that, planted in earth,

nurtured by water and by sun,

it would grow into something as huge and as magnificent

as a tree,

would you believe me?

So, too, can it be

with your dreams...

If your dynamic energy is blocked from flowing one way,

it is but an opportunity to find another course:

The river always wants to find its ocean.

The path is always choice;

choose to choose again;

never failure.

Be Still

When we are at peace within ourselves,

centred and empowered we are,

within our own uniqueness.

The journey of a thousand searches

stops

at the door to within...

Heed the stillness...

for inward lies strength.

Correcting Your Course

Mistakes are but points of correction
that give us direct guidance
on how to improve.

For someone's criticism to cut deep, we have to be agreeing.
And the stronger our reaction, the greater
the mutual accord.
For it is to the core of our self-disapproval that
their criticism is striking.
But when of our own selves we totally approve, no more can
their criticism smite.
Instead, we will glean only the useful potential and of it
avail as we head upon
our highest course.

Absorb what you need to absorb,
and disregard the rest.

If you have not achieved something extraordinary,
and yet have had a strong desire to do so,
it may be because you are not nurturing and
supporting yourself.
For when enjoyment and achievement go hand in hand,
the extraordinary becomes the best
of ordinary.

Caught up in expectations so demanding,
forget not that within each moment,
is the pleasure
of living.

One can only ever be as gentle
or as angry with another
as you are with yourself.

If you think you are doing someone a favour,
and they constantly let you down,
ask yourself,
'On whose knee does the need fall?'

Enjoy what you achieve,
and achieve
what you enjoy.

Without focus
There can be no direction.

The greater the perspective,
the easier it is to see
the whole.

A Step to the Lateral

Why be the thousandth hand knocking upon
a well-worn door, when you can flow through
a doorway that was
never
really there...

Often in simplicity
lies
the greatest meaning.

The more you think you know,
the less you are likely
to discover...

When you are up against a 'problem,'

you are giving it solid form.

But launch yourself upon an outcome,

becoming one with the alchemy of flow,

and the obstacled course will turn

to stream...

Support

The more angry you are with yourself,
the more likely you are to hear the angry,
self-hating voice that demands what
you should do *now!*

But the more gentle you are with yourself,
the more you will hear that gentle, loving voice
that guides...

Be intimate with yourself first.
Give to yourself what you've always wanted to receive
from others
and the balance of intimacy with another
then becomes not so hard
to attain.

Focus on what you most want to do,
and those who will most support you
will appear upon your path.

Another's grand success, or even tiny realisation, be they,
friend or acquaintance, is always full worth the celebration.
And every time you give your love and support
unconditionally, it is you who are the honoured.
For the more of others you affirm, the more nourished
your heart becomes, helping you transform into a vehicle
of purest love, without desire
for self-validation.

What I can do by myself
is multiplied exponentially
by what I can do with others.

...And Gratitude.

There is great humility in gratitude,
for it acknowledges all the love, care and support
from sources great and small,
that you received along your way.
But it is of humility transcendent when
under the light of gratitude, you acknowledge
all experiences and all people, irrespective of their nature,
who have partaken with you of life.

To yearn always for perfection in another;
to desire always perfection in yourself,
and to demand that of your life-path,
is to wallow in non-acceptance of a life
that is by nature imperfect,
making of your journey one rigid punishment.

Yet cleansed of this self-demand, and you are free at last to realise life's pleasure and to grace all that has succoured you with gratitude and joy.

Compassion Seeds

You can stay in the beaten child of mind's illusion.
Or you can grow into the powerful, compassionate being,
the Warrior of the Heart, that is:
You.
Ever potent is that promise...

Do not harden your heart to suffering.
Rather, open yourself up to the love,
joy and compassion
of connection.

Beyond the ego-lure of knowledge, intellect
and even seeming wisdom...
is the compassion
and the immensity
of unconditional love.

Speak your truth,
but say it with compassion.

True power

births

compassion.

Healing Balm

All healing

starts

within.

If you want to heal the World

heal yourself first,

then decide.

Heal the inner you,
and your outer world will follow.

You *don't* have to give people anything.
Loving them is enough.

If you are desperately trying to heal someone
who is not healing,
look within.
For that is where the desperate cry for help
is coming from.

Wounds heal.
And so can you.

Much misunderstood is the metaphysics of healing,
For healing of the most incurable can only ever take place
at the deepest and most loving of spiritual levels,
when Mind, Body and Spirit unify upon an instant,
in healing realisation.
Metaphysics is simply a guide, never spectre of blame,
nor of guilt
for such was always the ego's realm;
and do you know of anyone successfully punished
back to health?

When Spirit is ready to cure the Body,
it will attract
all that is necessary
to bring about the healing.

It is the love
not the words
that help the healing.

We are the choice.
We are the power.
We are the will,
that changes _all_ within.

Step follows step,
on the path to well-being.

Growing Greater Acceptance

We can have all the approval we ever sought,
twenty-four hours a day,
every second of the day.
All we have to do is ask

Ourselves.

We are who we are,
and we are the only ones
who can make ourselves acceptable
to ourselves.

If someone disapproves of you,
it is merely a challenge to approve of yourself.
So, do you have it within you,
To do just that?

You are not your years of age.
But you *are* your years of growth!

I know I can trust you
because I trust myself.

I know I can know you
because I know myself.

I know I can love you
because I love
myself...

Trying to see yourself through another's eyes
is like looking at yourself in a mirror.
So, look not. Believe the best is true.
And that...
will be reflected.

Accept and enjoy.

Not analyse and destroy.

Thou art Beautiful

in the eyes

of

thine own Beholder.

Accepting Others

Stand in wisdom over no woman, man.
For we are kin to all.

The illusion of separateness is the greatest of all dividers,
dividing human against human, belief from belief,
nation against nation, humanity from the Earth,
from kinship with all life forms
and from our Spiritual Essence.
Yet all who live are full capable of loving, yearning,
tears and laughter, and of our children caring.
And all of us do a similar body inhabit;
irrespective the colour of skin or the shape of a face.
And every one of us breathes the same air;
for is it not on this planet's life-nurture that
every living thing must depend?
So look not at another and think them different.
Instead, acknowledge that common bond between us:
For we are all of the human ... kind.

What we are strongly attracted to in others
is but a reminder of aspects of ourselves.
But so, too, are those qualities
that we most dislike.

The challenge to all who to a belief or faith hold strong
is to transcend surface difference,
go beyond the fear that holds us separate,
and lovingly accept
another's being.

Do not judge the path of experience
that others choose,
for they tread the path
of their own greatest learning.

Experience

An experience is like a waterfall:
Not by words will it be caught,
nor will come close the vehicle of mind,
so deceive yourself not by the language of Intellect,
For by being,
it is.

Where you are now
would not be,
but for the foundation
of where you have been.

Every experience is new,
so enjoy its freshness.
Do not compare it with the old.

Experience

anchors understanding

to the heart.

Wisdom's Song

The skein of Knowledge
can hide
the veil of Wisdom.

Those who have true wisdom, live, experience and feel it,
deep to the very heart of their being.
Enormous their humility, for they allow a wisdom
far greater than Self
its expression.

Beside the still pool
blossoms
the flower of Wisdom.

The chalice of wisdom is a thing blessed,
hidden not from the child within.

Of Essence

When we come from Essence, we are at centre

within our being.

Ruled no longer by guilt and fear wrenching us headfirst

into ego illusion,

our balance constantly adjusts as we seamlessly respond

to every input.

What stops you from being loving?

Nothing.

What is your purpose in life?

To be yourself.

What is your ultimate purpose?

Life.

The Child Within

Let the child lead and absorb what it will of Logic,
not let the Logic lead, deny, suppress and punish the child.
For the child within is truly a wonderful gift,
the mother and father of all creative invention,
that can travel worlds far beyond the imagination
of that caterpillar:
Logic.

You can spend your life trying to be an adult,
only to discover that
to be truly an adult
you also need to be
as a child.

There is joy in the spontaneous child:
Every gesture is alive
with the warmth of the giving,
and the pleasure derived.

Love the children, for they are love asking only
for its reflection,
reminding us adults all of what most have forgotten:
That maturity's full grace is both adult and child.
And what joy it can be to share the fun of aliveness
with those who are children, gently influencing each other
as we mature on our own journey towards true adulthood.
And though the Children of Now carry sway
beyond our years and may follow our example,
becoming beacons for generations yet unborn,
there is writ high, here, today, on every occasion we have,
opportunity to love
without desire for return.

Fun

It is safe to feel.
It is safe to want.
And it is *fun* to ask!

If you're a square peg,
<u>demand</u> a square hole!
You deserve the best.

If you talk to yourself,
isn't it good to know
that you are talking to somebody
equally as intelligent as yourself?

If you have misplaced something that you can never find,

you have clearly placed it somewhere top secret.

So secret that even you have no idea where it is.

It's in the ever-present moment

that we live our lives.

So let's enjoy life like a present

given every moment!

Beauty

Beauty lies within;
a far-shadowed tenderness reaching
all it beholds.

Beauty is joy at oneness,
solitary in the space of stillness.

Beauty is the warmth of a sunlit Spring,
in the chill of winter's dawns, as Nature heralds in
one new cycle.
For beauty is in all seasons of being.

Beauty is caring without possessing,
accepting without inhibiting,
even if their growth is towards shores by you unenvisioned;
never to feel your tread.

Beauty is in the joy of a child as it gives,
And in the heart of all who receive.

And beauty is in friendship, in the kindness of a smile,
the warmth of an eye.

And beauty is in touching, skin against skin,
body held in the warmth of another in soft dewed caress.

Beauty is in God's sweet grace,
Whatever be the Name.

Beauty,
unequalled and unfathomed,
is in each
and every breath
For beauty
is
the all-encompassed gift

of living.

Just Be

Inner certainty:
born
of inner knowing.

Trust.
The perfect people arrive
at the perfect time.

There is no judgement.
You are always contributing
to the Greater Scheme.
Just be.

Walk
in the silence
of your mind's creating.

The Next Step

There is potential within potential,

resource beyond resource,

knowledge transcendent of all knowing,

that is always there

for us.

Empower the positive.

Empower the light.

Empower only that born of love.

For such it is,

your soul purpose.

Create,

not await,

the time of readiness.

Often in that which you greatest fear,

Yet yearn to do,

bides your greatest challenge

for growth.

Find your passion, your joy,

then make of it your life message,

daubing it in multi-wondered splendour

across the vast canvas of the Universe.

Do not hold back.

Step with courage

towards the new.

On Track

When your life flows,

be at one.

No need to understand.

Guiding Others

Be the catalyst for other great hearts
to emerge from the cocoon of limitation.
Be the will that is

You.

When you offer guidance,
remember!
You are the planter of seeds.
And the seed will only germinate when
and if
the soil is ready.

On Mastery

The real path-finders through life
need no one's approval
to be exactly what they are:
catalysts
that others may follow.

One is not *made* a master.
One is a Master
whose time has come.

Let there be no more
the need for 'Spiritual Masters';
the very term redundant!
For all People will be in communion
with that immensity of Spiritual Love
and will, upon an instant,
empower their own healing.

Discovery

We are all creative.

For where there is joy in the doing,

there is creativity.

If you haven't yet tapped into that immensity, power

and grace that comes from sallying forth

on grand new endeavour,

then discover how!

Creativity is like intuition.

The more you acknowledge, play with, and explore it,

the more it will blossom.

Anything that sparks you,

listen and store.

For that spark could be the one

that ignites the flame of inspiration.

Dreams are the cool nucleus of mystery,

of *Magic illusioned,*

cascading us through and beyond the realm of walls,

<u>deep</u>

to the inner Source...

Capture, and be captivated by the ever potent spark

of new possibilities.

Discovery

lasts a lifetime...

Creed of the Evolution

If the vision fades, don't give in!
If the dream shatters, don't let up!
Blinded, fooled, lost and confused humanity may seem, but till
the breath departs us, our steps must walk the path of change.
For each step could be a foothold closer to that most cherished
of outcomes, for which survival is only impetus and part;
a purpose for unifying that will communion bring.

History led us to the present foundations,
with co-operation the generator of our salvation.
We who live now bear the challenge,
entrusted with a mission that knows no equal
in the annals of humanity.

Though days of darkness may precede us,
and voices fearing be raised in clamour;
Hearken not, for in the shadows of crisis
which so threatens every lifeform on our Globe,
grows a ground-swell ever more powerful,
many people uniting together in that greatest revolution:
the Evolution at last
of a Planetary Soul.

Long out of rhythm with the heart-breath of the Land,
imbued with vision redundant of civilised generations
unthinking of a world limitless in its supply,
all too inevitable was
this Earth crisis.

Yet all this is simply the progress that has steered humanity
near-sighted to the point that is now.
But the road before us turns, with change the only option.
Never before has humanity had to think so globally,
beyond person, or nation;
And with it is thrust the opportunity to seize the imperative,
creating from the old a new World Order,
eco-logical and co-operative.

As in wars, men and women of a nation rally together
in Common Cause, so now, in the artificial peace
of rich nations by nuclear peril created, lies a vastness
of new opportunities for understanding and growth.
And the networks are there: communication's link never forged
more strongly, nor the transport so fast.
By such means, initiatives and knowledge from high science
to the ground-roots, from spiritual wisdoms of cultures ancient
to developments the most modern, can throughout the World
be spread: humanity learning and relying on each other
as never before.

And was it not the migration of ideas from another spark,
infinitely smaller, that caused the Renaissance flame to
become the light across Medieval Europe?

Wait not for the short-term thinkers to realise change is needed;
Instead, awaken within to the vision of Whole Planet,
and from small or great a position, from one catalyst or many,
from tiny group to large organisation, keep or start the
momentum going, linking together all the islands:
For vital are the initiatives now.

To myself, and all who will listen,

Focus,

Focus on the light of healing change,

and let the love within you flow.

Of approval seek not, of comparisons ignore,

for you are tempered on the anvil of experience,

of a mettle yours unique.

Find your own voice, for your work is important,

leading your life in your own special way,

for no one can tell where your destiny may lead.

One voice may seem such a solitary sigh;

standing alone against a tidal wave direction.

Yet, one voice with clarity can be the resonance that

sets in motion transformation.

Learn from that force opposing you, its subtle flow,

Now, intuition guided, aim and, in seamless trust, soar,

to a lateral solution of the highest accord.

And from the tidal might that defies you will come

an answering echo; many voices adding to yours,

current-roaring into a crescendo of power,

surging as one

towards the most powerful of change.

Yet know that it is the love of what you do,
not the size, that matters.
Beware of 'should do' and 'must,' 'for others' sake' and
'for others' approval;'
for these are always ego-traps, and ultimately
the only one you can empower
is yourself.
Seek always the gentle call of peace within you, heeding
your intuition, for it will connect you to the source-flow of love,
and guide you upon your true path.
Of the light of Spirit, see as it shines through all people
that you meet within your day,
sharing with them in the joy of a smile.

And Nature, adore in all her magnificence, return to the
sacred knowing of the animal and plant, of every formation
of this Maternal Earth, recognising with the whole of our being
that we too are fully part of her wondrous creativity.
So, from ourselves to its every aspect, lovingly embrace
the spiritual perfection
of this Global Entity.

The more we attune with all our special gifts, the more our inner
glow does radiate – touching and inspiring.
And when our commitment is joyous, our inner connection
strong, it is with naturalness, grace and ease
that people will be drawn to us.
For one may never know how the far ripple of our presence
will extend beyond our near effect to benefit
all kind.

Through the Millennium gate, we tread a hazardous course,
with opportunity bolstering up our every step
towards tomorrows yet to come.
To the many, the power to make real change, as People
worldwide, irrespective of race or creed, do their activities
co-ordinate, working together upon our mutual necessity.
Magnificent too is the resource and insight accessed as women
realise the voice they deserve in the world;
embracing their power as equals.
For exponentially increased is the power to heal when
men and women stride out as one upon the quest,
global change.

To the challenges of adversity will arise leaders of greatness and
global vision to harness our energies combined.
And in such climate-productive, breakthroughs unimagined in
areas once unsolvable will occur, translating
into world reality at speeds untold.
For when we as a People commit to global responsibility
with clarity of intent; guidance phenomenal will awaken
into consciousness, co-creating a new reality
with unparalleled effect.

Always has humanity been supported on the deepest
of spiritual levels, the source of all inspiration and experience,
waiting with infinite patience the coming of humankind
into the ocean of co-existence.
For we are in truth spiritual journeyers and
this realm of free will;
our planetary school of learning.

As civilisation arose and spread, we as a species
entered our adolescence, bringing to an end
the million-year walk of the Nomad.
But as a result, the Essence Feminine that had nurtured us for

so long, bathing us in a deep connectedness to Earth Mother,
became submerged beneath an Essence Masculine
grown dominant.
Myriad were the paths the strands of our race explored, but
Nature we attempted to conquer and convert to suit ourselves,
and her needs were forgotten.

Yet vast has been the learning, and the foundation created;
even through the chaos of wars, the demise of species, and
the environmental havoc we have wrought during these,
our formative years. For in the realm of Spirit
there are no atrocities, only the infiniteness
of compassion,
as soul learns from soul and from Nature
in order to evolve.

Always has there been a truer purpose beyond that which
humanity perceived, for, though disunited, we are now
interconnected with our minds and knowledge pooled
as never before.
We face now the exact catalyst that will propel us forward
into a global evolution in consciousness;
the Earth in crisis.

The task ahead, heralding our adulthood as a species,
is to reconnect to the Earth with a much deeper sensitivity,
assuming the mantle that has long awaited us;
the Custodians of our Planet.
And it is now that the deep Earth wisdom of the
Essence Feminine is reassuming its rightful place alongside the
Essence Masculine, illuminating the road before us with
the brilliance of intuition.

By accepting that at the heart of all our species lies the concern
for future generations, then, individually and collectively,
we are empowering our spiritual evolution and fulfilling that
inherent potential, the birth vision within every one of us
of becoming instrumental
in the Global healing.

As the Evolution gains momentum, it will be found that
there is not One True Path, but many a way equally valid.
There will be those who cling to the old, and those pushing
forward to the new, yet from their variance will
be resolved an unheard-of new dynamic.
The more the branches of human endeavour join in

Common Cause, the higher still the extraordinary synergy,
as interdependence, nation with nation,
becomes the new meaning in the Land.
And one by one, old structures will fall or give way
to their greater purpose as the voice, once small,
becomes the World.

...And a Final Thought

Let the best impress.

Epilogue

And so, my friends, concludes this book of my sayings. And if they have given you, like me, cause for reflection, moments worth cherishing, or a knowing nod, then I am gratified. Thank you for sharing my journey of insight through the experience of life.

Adrian

Acknowledgements:

With grateful thanks to the following; To my wife, friends and family for all their love, inspiration and support over the years.

With grateful thanks to the following; To my wife, friends and family for all their love, inspiration and support over the years.

To all those who helped this mammoth project come into being. These include early influences, authors Shakti Gawain, Louise Hay and Sondra Ray, and seminar leaders Robert Kiyosaki, Jan Gauvin and Diane McCann. Also to Reiki masters, Beth Gray, Alma Devi, Denise Crundall as well as to friends Grant Richter and Cath McDowall. A special thanks to Elaine Foster-Massie for providing the impetus for the book and to Susan Hayward, author and editor of *A Guide for the Advanced Soul*, for her gentle, enthusiastic encouragement at an important early stage. Without these two people, it is unlikely that this book would even have been created.

And last but not least, thank you to that ultimate source, whatever be the name.

About the Author

Adrian is a screenwriter, actor and novelist. Born in England in 1955, he emigrated to Australia with his family as a child. As well as writing several feature film scripts, he has written a number of novels. They range from children's novels, inspirational sayings to comedy and psychological thrillers. Together with travelling to multiple countries, Adrian has had over twenty different jobs, from delivering babies, teaching asylum seekers English, video editing, taxi driving and Reiki mastership. He was a Registered nurse/midwife for nearly forty years, including working in the outback and in prisons. He is married and now retired from his role as an officer of the courts in Adelaide, South Australia. More about Adrian can be found at: www.theworksofadriancrawford.com

"I have an inquisitive mind, a caring nature, and a gentle sense of humour capable of seeing the foibles of human nature, including my own. My thirties were very much an apprenticeship, with this, my largest project to that time, a most suitable summation."

Adrian Crawford, 2021

www.ingramcontent.com/pod-product-compliance
Lightning Source LLC
Chambersburg PA
CBHW021154080526
44588CB00008B/339